Can You Count the Critters?

by Stan Tekiela

Adventure Publications
Cambridge, Minnesota

Dedication

To the children of the world. Stand up and be counted.

Photos by Stan Tekiela

Edited by Sandy Livoti
Cover and book design by Jonathan Norberg

10 9 8 7 6 5 4 3

Can You Count the Critters?
Copyright © 2019 by Stan Tekiela
Published by Adventure Publications
An imprint of AdventureKEEN
310 Garfield Street South
Cambridge, Minnesota 55008
(800) 678-7006
www.adventurepublications.net
Printed in China
ISBN 978-1-59193-819-4 (pbk.)

Can You Count the Critters?

This butterfly is a beautiful insect. It flies south for the winter.

Butterflies begin their lives as eggs. The eggs hatch into tiny caterpillars. The caterpillars later turn into butterflies.

Monarch

Toads have bumpy skin and look like brown frogs. They live on land and water.

2 Can you count the toads?

Male toads sing very loud songs in spring. Their throats get big when they sing.

American Toad

Eastern Cottontail

Baby rabbits have cute, pointed ears and small, fluffy white tails.

They are fast runners!
They zigzag back and forth
when they are chased.

3 Can you count the rabbits?

American Black Bear

These bears are not always black. They can be many different colors.

Bears are covered with soft fur and have big, round ears.

4 Can you count the bears?

5 Can you count the prairie dogs?

Prairie dogs live in families.
Each family may have
more than five pups.

Lots of prairie dog families live close together. Young prairie dog brothers and sisters often kiss each other to say hello.

Black-tailed Prairie Dog

ELK are just like deer, only much larger. In the fall, the dads call very loudly, making sounds like a horn.

The moms gather together to protect the babies. Baby elk have white spots on their fur.

Elk

6 Can you count the elk?

Can you count the eagles?

These eagles are the biggest eagles in the U.S. and Canada. The adults have white heads and tails.

During winter they gather in groups and go fishing. Sometimes they stand, or perch, together on a log.

Bald Eagle

Newborn opossums grow in a pouch on their mom's belly. When they get bigger, they ride on her back. They hold on tightly to keep from falling off.

Virginia Opossum

Opossums have five short pink toes. They use their tails to grip branches when they climb around in trees.

8 Can you count the opossums?

These bats have longer noses and tongues than other bats. At night they visit flowers to feed on sweet nectar, their favorite food.

Lesser Long-nosed Bat

9 Can you count the bats?

Bats are the only mammals that fly.

10

Can you count the turtles?

These turtles are the most common turtle in the U.S. and Canada. Their bright yellow and orange markings look like paintings on their necks and shells.

In the summer, turtles climb on logs to warm up in the sun. Sitting in sunlight also helps them digest their food.

Painted Turtle

This duck might be the most common duck in the world. The adult females can lay ten eggs.

11

Can you count the ducks?

Little ducklings follow their mom to the water one day after they hatch and swim with her right away.

Mallard

Bison are also called buffalo. They are some of the largest animals in the U.S. and Canada. Grown males can weigh almost as much as a car!

American Bison

12

Can you count the bison?

Baby bison have rusty red
fur when they are born.
They run and follow the group,
or herd, right after birth.

1 Monarch

The Monarch is one of the few butterflies that regularly migrate long distances at the end of summer. Most spend the winter in California and in the mountains of Mexico. In spring, they fly north to mate. Monarch females lay eggs only on milkweed plants. Monarch caterpillars eat milkweed leaves and nothing else.

2 American Toad

The American Toad is one of the most common amphibians in the U.S. and Canada. Toads have dry, bumpy skin and live mostly on land, unlike frogs. Frogs have smooth skin and live mostly in water. Toads have short legs and hop short distances. Frogs have long legs and leap longer distances.

3 Eastern Cottontail

Eastern Cottontails are the most common rabbit in the U.S. and Canada. They usually rest under a bush during the day. At night they come out to eat and play. Moms give birth to up to twelve babies. Bunnies stay in the nest for just two weeks. After leaving the nest, they are able to take care of themselves.

4 American Black Bear

American Black Bears are the most common bear in the U.S. and Canada. Despite their name, some of these bears are brown or rusty red. Others are even white! The adult males are much larger and heavier than the females. Bears can see and hear better than people. Their sense of smell is seven times better than a dog's.

5 Black-tailed Prairie Dog

Black-tailed Prairie Dogs are a type of squirrel. They live in burrows underground in prairies and deserts. Their burrows have many entrances and exits. Prairie dogs have different calls, and they understand each other very well. They can warn their community about a predator approaching and communicate about its size and location.

6 Elk

Elk are members of the deer family. They live in forested areas and prairies. The adult males have two large antlers on their heads. Large antlers show the females that the males are strong and healthy. The antlers drop off once each year, and soon new ones start to grow.

7 Bald Eagle

The Bald Eagle is a large raptor that is found only in the U.S. and Canada. It has white feathers on its head and huge yellow feet. It has long toes and sharp nails, called talons. Eagles use their feet to catch prey. Of all North American birds, eagles build the largest nests, reaching ten feet wide and ten feet tall!

8 Virginia Opossum

Opossums have long, naked tails. Sometimes small, young opossums use their tails to hang upside down in trees. The adults are too heavy to do this. Like kangaroos, opossums are marsupials. Marsupial moms keep their babies close and warm on their bellies in a fur-lined pouch. Opossums are the only marsupials in the U.S. and Canada.

9 Lesser Long-nosed Bat

Lesser Long-nosed Bats use their long tongues to lap up nectar in flowers that bloom at night. Bats have excellent vision, especially in dim light. They fly with their hands, not their arms. Thin, flexible skin between each of their fingers stretches out to create their wings.

10 Painted Turtle

Painted Turtles feed on aquatic plants, aquatic insects and fish. The females are larger than the males, but the males have much larger front claws. When you see a turtle walking across a road during summer, it's usually a female. She is heading to a place to lay and bury her eggs.

11 Mallard

The breeding male Mallard is much more colorful than the female. After each breeding season, the male sheds his bright feathers and looks like the female. Male Mallards don't quack. Only the females call the typical loud "quack, quack, quack." Mallards eat mostly green plants and roots. Aquatic insects make up the rest of their diet.

12 American Bison

American Bison have a long, shaggy coat of fur that keeps them warm during winter. In summer they have a much shorter, cooler coat. The adult males have huge heads and a large dark mane of fur. They can be twice the size of females! Bison usually feed for about two hours, and then sit down to rest.

About the Author

STAN TEKIELA

Naturalist, wildlife photographer and writer Stan Tekiela is the originator of the popular Wildlife and Nature Appreciation book series that includes *Bird Migration* and *Wildflowers*. Stan has authored more than 190 educational books, including field guides, quick guides, nature books, children's books, playing cards and more, presenting many species of animals and plants.

With a Bachelor of Science degree in Natural History from the University of Minnesota and as an active professional naturalist for more than 30 years, Stan studies and photographs wildlife throughout the United States and Canada. He has received various national and regional awards for his books and photographs. Also a well-known columnist and radio personality, his syndicated column appears in more than 25 newspapers, and his wildlife programs are broadcast on a number of Midwest radio stations. Stan can be followed on Facebook and Twitter. He can be contacted via www.naturesmart.com.

MORE CHILDREN'S BOOKS FROM STAN

Stan Tekiela's books for children feature gorgeous photographs of real animals paired with captivating text. They introduce children to common, interesting and important types of North American animals.

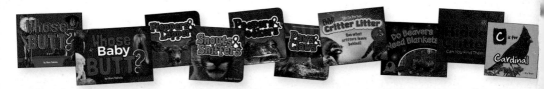